Face
to
Face

WOLVES

DATE DUE

11-13-14

Q2AMedia

Created by Q2AMedia
www.q2amedia.com
Text, design & illustrations Copyright © 2009 Q2AMedia

Editor Honor Head and Jean Coppendale
Publishing Director Chester Fisher
Art Director Sumit Charles
Senior Designers Joita Das, Prashant Kumar and Shilpi Sarkar
Project Manager Shekhar Kapur

Illustrators Subhash Vohra and Stanley Morrison
Art Editor Sujatha Menon
Picture Researcher Iti Shrotriya

an imprint of
SCHOLASTIC
www.scholastic.com

Published by Tangerine Press, an imprint of Scholastic Inc., 557 Broadway, New York, NY 10012

Scholastic Canada Ltd.; Markham, Ontario

Scholastic Australia Pty. Ltd; Gosford NSW

Scholastic New Zealand Ltd.; Greenmount, Auckland

10 9 8 7 6 5 4 3 2 1

ISBN: 0-545-23691-1

Printed in Shenzhen, China

Picture Credits
t=top, tr=top right, tl=top left, bl= bottom left, br=bottom right, b=bottom

Cover Images (All): Ralph Roach: Shutterstock. Back Cover: Q2AMedia Art Bank.

Title Page: Sebastien Gauthier: Shutterstock Imprint Page: Eric Isselée: Shutterstock. Half title: Len Tillim: Istockphoto

Contents Images: **4t** Leo Kowal: Istockphoto. **4b** Markus Divis: Istockphoto. **5t** Shutterstock. **5b** Eduard Kyslynskyy: Istockphoto.

6 Lukasz Chyrek: Istockphoto. **8** Photostogo. **9** Kevin R Morris: Corbis. **10-11** Matt Patterson: Photolibrary. **10** Jonathan Lyons/Istockphoto. **11** Morales Morales: Photolibrary. **12-13** Jeanne Drake: Photolibrary. **12** John Banagan: Lonely Planet Images. **13** Pixshots: Shutterstock. **14-15** Jurgen Freund: Nature Picture Library. **15** Denis Pepin: Shutterstock. **16-17** Eyal Bartov: Photolibrary. **16** Earl Robbins: Fotolia. **17** Andrew Harrington: Nature Picture Library. **18-19** Manfred Delpho: Photolibrary. **19** Michael Sewell: Photolibrary. **20** Leo Kowal: Istockphoto. **21t** Jim Brandenburg: Minden Pictures: FLPA. **21b** J&C Sohns: Photolibrary. **22** Ronald Wittek: Photolibrary. **24** Douglas Smith: NPS. **26-27** White: Photolibrary. **27** Jim Brandenburg: Minden Pictures: FLPA. **28-29** D.Robert Franz: Corbis. **29** Henry Ausloos: Photolibrary. **30-31** Ronald Wittek: Photolibrary. **31t** Holly Kuchera: Istockphoto.

31b Martin Harvey: Photolibrary. **32** Daniel Cox: Photolibrary. **34-35** Anup Shah: Nature Picture Library. **35** Hans Proppe: Istockphoto. **36-37** Gordon&Cathy Illg: Photolibrary. **37** Jim Brandenburg: Minden Pictures: FLPA. **38** Michael Weber: Photolibrary. **39t** J&C Sohns: Photolibrary. **39b** David W Middleton: Photolibrary. **40-41** Manfred Delpho: Photolibrary. **40** Les Stocker: Photolibrary. **42-43** Joe Blossom: NHPA: Photoshot. **42** Stephen Krasemann: NHPA. **44** Johan Swanepoel: Shutterstock. **45l** Ewan Chesser: Shutterstock. **45r** Geoffrey Kuchera: Shutterstock. **46-47** Ron Hilton: Shutterstock. **48** Sebastien Gauthier: Shutterstock.

Q2AMedia Art Bank: **6, 7, 23, 25, 33.**

WOLVES

Sally Morgan

Contents

Gray wolf

Arctic wolves

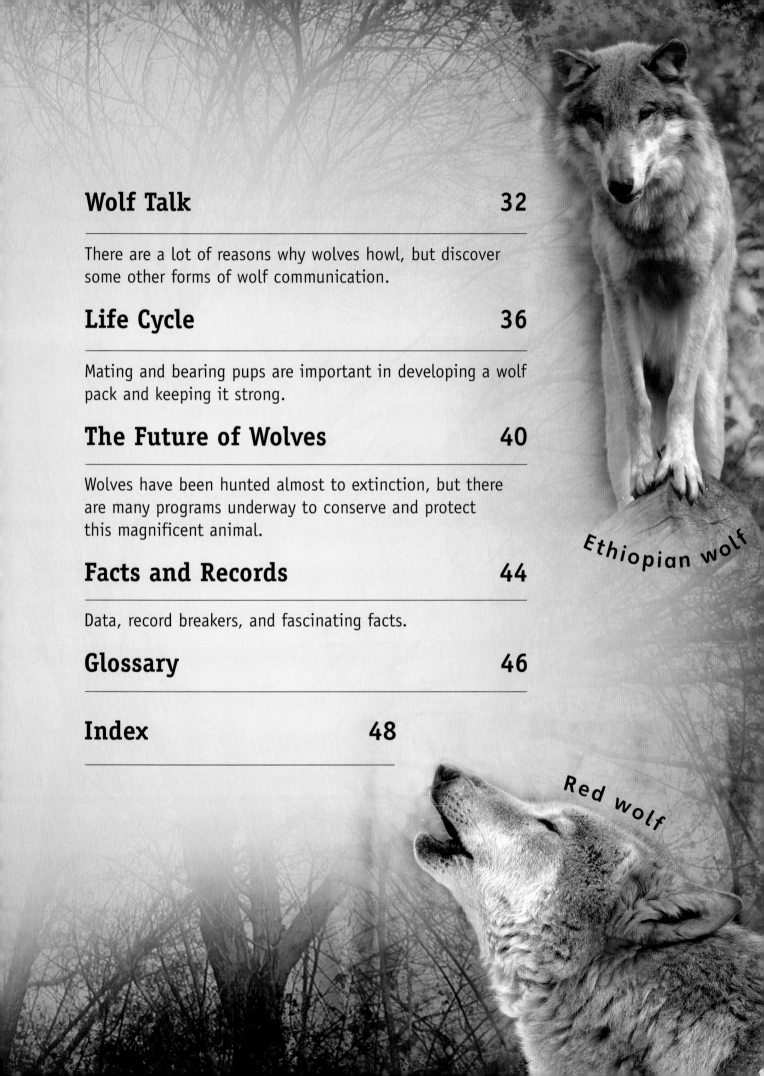

Ethiopian wolf

Red wolf

Master Hunters

A spine-chilling howl echoes through the thick, dark trees.
This is the sound of the wolf, one of the most feared
animals of the northern forests.

Living in a pack

The wolf is the largest member of the dog family
and once roamed widely across the northern
hemisphere. Today, many types, or species, of
wolf have declined or disappeared. Wolves are
social animals that live in a group called a pack.
When pups are born, all the members of the
pack help to look after the young.

◄ *Many wolves howl at sunset. In open countryside,
their howls can carry for up to 9 mi. (15 km).*

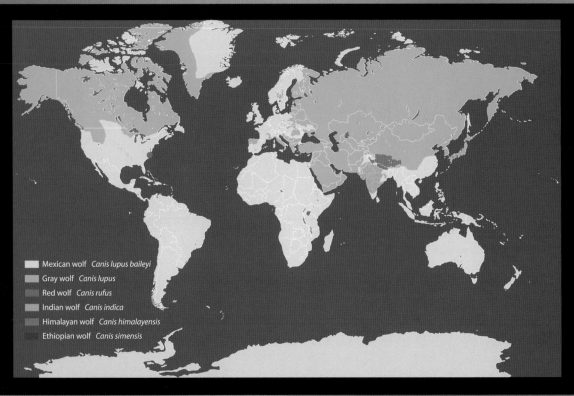

Mexican wolf *Canis lupus baileyi*
Gray wolf *Canis lupus*
Red wolf *Canis rufus*
Indian wolf *Canis indica*
Himalayan wolf *Canis himalayensis*
Ethiopian wolf *Canis simensis*

◄ *Wolves have adapted
to many different
habitats. They live in the
cold conifer forests of
North America and
Europe, mountain ranges,
the hot deserts of the
Middle East and Ethiopia,
and the wilderness of
central Asia. The smallest
and lightest in color,
the Arabian wolves, are
found in the desert, and
the largest, the tundra
wolves, are found in
the Arctic.*

Upright ears.

The body of the wolf is designed for long-distance running to chase prey. Wolves have a narrow chest, long back, and muscular legs. They usually move around at a trot; that's faster than a walk but not as fast as a gallop.

Forward-looking eyes to spot prey.

Tail is about one quarter of the body length.

Powerful jaws for catching prey.

Small fifth claw, called a dewclaw, behind foot.

Front paw with four clawed toes.

Powerful back legs to push wolf forward.

▲ Wolves are powerful predators that hunt other animals, even animals much larger than themselves, such as this moose.

Meat eaters

The wolf is a mammal. There are thousands of species of mammals. Carnivores are meat-eating mammals. Wolves and other members of the dog family are carnivores. Other well-known carnivores include cats, bears, raccoons, and stoats.

Hunted and trapped

Wolves rarely attack humans. They will only attack if threatened or when they are protecting their young. However, wolves hunt farm animals, especially sheep and goats. For this reason wolves have been hunted, trapped, and even poisoned by farmers. Huge wolf packs are now greatly reduced in size.

Wolves and people

In North America, wolves play an important role in Native American culture, where they represent strength, endurance, and loyalty. Long ago, some Native American tribes dressed in wolf skins to hunt, while others refused to kill a wolf in case it brought bad luck. The people of the Pawnee tribe are often called the "wolf people" because of their close relationship with the wolf. The hand signal that they use to introduce themselves as Pawnee also means "wolf."

Eagle feathers.

Wolf's head.

▶| *This man from the Arapaho tribe is wearing a war bonnet made from a wolf's head and eagle feathers. His face is painted to give the appearance of a wolf.*

Worldwide
Wolves

The gray wolf is found in the forests of North America, Europe and Asia. But there are other species of wolf found around the world, including the red wolf and the Ethiopian wolf.

Gray wolf

The gray wolf is the largest and best-known of the wolves. Most have a gray coat as their name suggests, but the color ranges from a dark gray and black to almost pure white. There are slight differences in the appearance of gray wolves living in different parts of the world. These wolves are given different names—for example, the European, Iranian, Tundra, and Mexican wolf.

Red wolf

The red wolf is smaller than the gray wolf and has particularly large ears. The red wolf gets its name from its reddish-brown coat. It has gray and black hairs along its back and head, with a distinctive white edge to the mouth.

◄ *The red wolf is very rare and only found in a few places in the United States.*

Ethiopian wolf

The slender, long-legged Ethiopian wolf looks more like a red fox than a wolf, but scientists have discovered that it is closely related to the gray wolf. This reddish wolf, with black and white marks on the head and tail, weighs just about 35 lbs. (16 kg). It is only found in the mountains of Ethiopia.

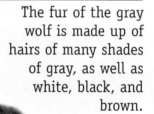

Long hairs over the shoulders make the wolf look larger.

The fur of the gray wolf is made up of hairs of many shades of gray, as well as white, black, and brown.

⊼ *The Ethiopian wolf has a reddish coat and a long muzzle.*

⊼ *The gray wolf is found in the wilderness regions of North America and parts of Europe and Asia.*

Dingoes

The wolf's closest relatives are dingoes, jackals, and pet dogs. Dingoes and jackals are smaller than wolves and are found in different parts of the world. The dingo is a wild dog found in the harsh deserts of Australia and parts of Southeast Asia. It has a reddish-brown coat with white markings. Dingoes have descended from the gray wolf, and scientists think they came to Australia with the first Aborigines.

◀ *A dingo is the size of a medium pet dog but has a longer muzzle.*

Jackal scavengers

Jackals are found in Africa and across the Middle East to South Asia. They are cunning predators that hunt at night. Sometimes they scavenge for food, feeding on dead animals and remains left by other predators. They also eat fruits and berries. Silver-backed jackals usually live together, either in pairs or in small family groups.

⏷ *This family of silver-backed jackals has found the remains of a dead animal.*

⏴ *The many different breeds of dog, from the Great Dane to the tiny Chihuahua, have all descended from the gray wolf.*

Pet dogs

People first kept dogs more than 15,000 years ago. Nobody is sure whether the first pet dogs were abandoned wolf cubs or just wolves that liked to live close to people. The wolf was one of the few animals that was not scared of people, and it used to look for food around settlements. These clever animals may have begged for food and become tame.

Desert and Snow

Wolves are found in a variety of habitats, from scorching deserts and grasslands to forests and mountains. They are even found in the sub-zero temperatures of the Arctic. Wolves vary in size and color according to where they live.

Cold homes

Most wolves are found in forests, especially the conifer forests of North America and Europe, where they can find prey, such as caribou and deer. They also inhabit the vast frozen tundra of the Arctic, where they have to cope with extreme cold and long, dark days in winter.

Arctic survivors

The Arctic wolves have a white coat that provides excellent camouflage in the snow. The coat is thick, too, providing insulation against the cold. Hairs around the pads of their feet help keep them warm on the snowy ground. Arctic wolves cover long distances to find prey, and many follow herds of caribou as they journey south in winter.

▶| *The Arctic wolf grows an extra-thick coat in winter to survive the freezing conditions. When it sleeps, it curls up tightly and pulls its tail around its face.*

⌖ *A pack of gray wolves makes its way through deep snow covering a forest.*

Mexican wolf

The Mexican wolf is slender with long legs. Its coat is mostly gray with light brown hairs along the back. It is found in the mountains of the southwestern United States. Numbers of this type of wolf have fallen, and it is now protected by law.

◄ *The Mexican wolf is the smallest of the North American gray wolves and also the rarest.*

Big ears

One of the smallest wolves is the Arabian wolf, a type of grey wolf that is found in the deserts of the Middle East. It weighs just about 39 lbs. (18 kg). Its extra-large ears help it keep cool. Warm blood flowing around the big ears loses heat to the surrounding air. When this blood returns to the body, it is much cooler. The coat of the Arabian wolf is pale brown to yellow, with a hint of red, colors that blend well with the desert sand.

▲ *Unlike other grey wolves, the Arabian wolf does not usually form packs. Instead, it lives alone or with another wolf. It hunts smaller animals, such as rabbits, antelope, deer, and goats, that it can kill on its own.*

▶| *An Ethiopian wolf runs across a grassy plain in search of prey.*

Mountain homes

Some wolves, such as gray, Ethiopian, Indian, and Himalayan, live in the mountains. Ethiopian wolves are found in the highlands of Ethiopia, living on grassy slopes above the forests at altitudes of 11,480–12,465 ft. (3,500– 3,800 m) above sea level. They hunt small mammals, such as the giant mole rat.

Pack Life

Wolves live in packs. A pack is made up of a family group of 8 to 15 wolves, but some have as many as 20.

Pack leaders

A top male and female wolf, known as the alpha pair, lead each pack. They are the most experienced, and often oldest, wolves. The rest of the pack is made up of their offspring, close relatives, and sometimes unrelated wolves. When prey is scarce, a pack may enter another pack's territory and savage fights occur.

▼ *The dominant wolf (looking at camera) works hard to keep the rest of the wolf pack under control.*

Dominant wolf.

This wolf is lower in the pack ranking and is licking the muzzle of the dominant wolf.

This adult wolf is scent-marking a fallen tree trunk along the edge of the pack's territory.

Territory

The pack lives and hunts in an area called a territory. The size of the territory depends on the pack size and the amount of prey. In areas where prey is scarce, there are smaller packs that hunt over a much larger area. Wolves mark the boundaries of their territory by spraying their urine on boulders, bushes, and other obvious objects. This is called scent-marking.

FACT

One of the largest wolf packs ever seen was in Yellowstone National Park. In the "Druid Peak" pack, there were 37 wolves, including 21 cubs of varying ages. However, the pack was too large, and it broke up into three smaller packs. This was because they could not find enough food in their territory.

Pack position

The position of each wolf within the pack is carefully worked out. By having a pack order, there are fewer fights, because every wolf knows its position. A wolf's position in the pack determines what it can do. For example, only the alpha female is allowed to have pups. The other wolves in the pack help the alpha female raise and protect the pups, so that more survive.

▶| Lone wolves tend to be young males driven out from their family pack, looking for their own territory. When they find an area without other wolves, they can begin a pack of their own by taking a mate and having pups.

FACT

Wolves lick their wounds because their saliva contains substances that help reduce infection and speed up healing.

A dominant wolf chases away a lower-ranked wolf that tried to challenge its position in the pack.

Becoming alpha

Any wolf can become an alpha wolf. If the alpha male or female is injured or killed, the next highest wolf in the pack, the beta wolf, usually moves up to take its place. Sometimes, a newcomer takes the place of an alpha male or female that has died or is weak.

The alpha wolf

An alpha wolf decides where and what to hunt, and the other wolves follow its lead. The alpha wolf protects the pack when danger threatens. When there is plenty of food, the pack eats at the same time. But if there is limited food, the alpha pair and the young pups are first to feed.

The alpha wolves make sure the pups have plenty of food before allowing the rest of the pack to feed.

Keeping rank

All the wolves in a pack are ranked in order, from the alpha male and female at the top, to the omega male and female at the bottom. The rank order is established by carefully controlled fights between the wolves. The alpha wolf is not always the strongest wolf, but is the most dominant and best-suited to lead. Wolf fights are not always physical, and the wolves are not seriously injured. But there is a lot of growling and bullying between the wolves to work out which one has the higher rank.

Body language

Wolves communicate through their body language, such as facial expressions, body position, and the way they hold their tail. Scientists can determine a wolf's rank in the pack by watching how it interacts with other wolves. An alpha wolf stands more upright and holds its tail higher, compared with a lower-ranked wolf, which stoops more, hugs the ground, and holds its tail lower. If two wolves have a disagreement, they have a face-off. They try to look fierce by showing their teeth and growling.

The wolf on the left is the dominant wolf. Its eyes are staring at the wolf on the right, which has looked down.

When a lower-ranked wolf meets a higher-ranked wolf, it keeps its tail low and ears back. It bares its teeth in a grin, avoids staring at the other wolf, and may even roll over onto its back. This is called submissive behavior.

Tail raised.

Eyes staring directly at submissive wolf.

The dominant wolf has a threatening grin.

The submissive wolf has rolled onto its back.

Ears back.

Cunning Hunters

Wolves are hunters. They mainly feed on large animals, such as moose and caribou. However, if the opportunity arises, they will eat hares, birds, and other small animals, too.

Attack plan

Wolves are successful predators because they are flexible hunters, using different methods to catch their prey. Usually, the pack hunts together. Wolves pick the weaker animals in a herd, such as animals that are old, injured, or sick.

Strong jaws

Wolves have particularly strong jaws, which they need to hang on to their prey. Wolves also use their jaws to crush bones so they can get the bone marrow inside. Their razor-sharp canine teeth grip the prey and pull off meat. Behind the canines are large teeth with jagged edges that can slice through flesh.

▲ *This pack has surrounded a large buffalo. The wolves will leap up and attack its back legs with their claws and bite the animal with their teeth. The buffalo will be weakened before it collapses.*

Wolves are armed with razor-sharp teeth and claws to catch and eat their prey. Wolves do not chew their food. Instead, they tear it into large pieces, which they swallow whole.

Sometimes wolves attack other predators, such as bears. A pack of 12 wolves was able to surround and kill a grizzly bear.

FACT

A wolf has 42 teeth. There are 12 small incisors at the front of the mouth.

Dewclaw.

Each of the four canine teeth is between 0.7 and 1 in. (2 and 3 cm) in length.

The four clawed toes and the small dewclaw are used to grip food.

Easy prey

Wolves hunt the easiest prey: Those that are already weak. Over time, the prey animal species actually get stronger because only the healthiest survive to produce young. Wolves are expert hunters, but it is dangerous and not always successful. Sometimes the prey injures a wolf or gets away. Scientists studying one pack of wolves found that only one in every 12 hunts was successful.

▲ *These wolves are chasing an Arctic hare. Their extra-large front paws help to spread their weight so they don't sink into the snow.*

FACT

Wolves can trot effortlessly for many hours, covering a lot of ground in search of food. Some days they may travel as many as 62 mi. (100 km).

Hunting at night

Red wolves hunt at night, often on their own. They prey on small animals, such as white-tailed deer and raccoons, which they kill by themselves. If they are hungry, they eat birds, fish, and even snakes.

▼ *These Arctic wolves are chasing a group of musk oxen. These are dangerous animals to hunt because the wolves may be injured by the oxen's horns.*

Plenty of food

After a successful hunt, wolves gorge themselves on food. They can eat virtually the entire animal, including the bones and skin. They dig into the large muscles on the hind legs first. The organs, especially the liver and heart, are their favorite parts. They eat quickly, filling their stomach with as much as 24 lbs. (11 kg) of food at a time.

Farmers' enemy

Wolves find animals, such as goats, sheep, and even cattle, easy prey and will kill these animals for food. For this reason, wolves have never been popular with farmers. During the last few hundred years, thousands of wolves have been shot or trapped. Now people are finding ways to scare wolves away without killing them, such as using loud bangs or tying flags to fences.

▼ *These young wolf cubs are feeding on the remains of a dead animal.*

Scavengers

Wolves can survive several days without food. This is particularly important in winter when heavy snow can make hunting difficult. Sometimes, wolves bury their food and dig it up a few weeks later. If food is scarce, wolves will scavenge and feed on already dead animals and the remains of other animals' kills.

▲ *Little will be left of this kill after these hungry wolves have filled their stomachs.*

Super Senses

Wolves have excellent senses. Their senses of smell and hearing are particularly strong. These senses help them find their way around in the dark and seek out prey.

Smelling the world

A wolf's ability to smell is thought to be 100 times better than that of a human. Smell plays an important role in their lives. Wolves hunt downwind, that is, with the wind blowing toward them. This means that they can pick up the smell of their prey more easily.

Urine has a strong smell and wolves use it to mark their territory. Wolves can even identify other members of the pack from the smell of their urine.

FACT

Excellent eyesight

Wolves can see as well as humans in bright light, but at night their sight is far better. This helps them hunt in the dark. Their eyes are positioned so they look forward, like ours, giving them 3-D vision. They can also spot movement out of the corner of their eyes.

Large ears

Wolves have large earflaps that funnel sounds into their ears, giving the wolf hearing that is many times better than that of a human. They are particularly quick to hear high-pitched sounds. Wolves can also move their ears and even fold them back to hear better and to figure out where a sound is coming from.

Wolves use their excellent sense of smell to follow a scent trail that will lead them to their prey.

Wolf Talk

The sound of a lone wolf howling at night can be scary. Often other wolves will join in, and soon all the wolves in the neighborhood are howling. But why do wolves howl?

Social howling

Howling is the way wolves communicate with each other. Social howling is important for bonding between the members of a pack. When one wolf howls, the others join in, and this makes the bonds between the wolves stronger. Sometimes, wolves howl when they are resting as a warning to rival packs to stay away.

Hunting calls

Excited howling takes place at the start of a hunt when the wolves are eager to track prey. During the hunt, the members of the pack may scatter, so once hunting has ended, they howl again to bring the pack together. This howl is different—it is deep and loud, and often includes a few barks.

Pups start to howl within a few weeks of birth, and they practice their howls for the next couple of months.

In 1959, biologists working in a national park in Canada discovered that when they mimicked the howl of a wolf, a real wolf answered back! Now "talking to wolves" is a popular activity with summer visitors.

The howl of a lone wolf is long and eerie, with a wail at the end. It is often heard during the breeding season when a lone male wolf is searching for a female. For much of the time, a lone wolf is silent, because it does not want to be attacked by a pack.

Tell-tale howls

Wolves do not howl unnecessarily because it gives away their position. Packs learn a lot about other packs from listening to their howls—for example, the number of wolves in the pack and its location. With this information, the listening wolves may decide that they are the stronger pack and attack.

Staying clear

Sometimes, one pack replies to the howling of another pack. This may be to threaten the other pack, or simply to tell it where they are. This avoids the two packs bumping into each other while hunting and prevents a pack fight. But sometimes, a pack stays silent so it can creep up on another pack and steal its food.

▶ *These wolves are howling at the same time. Howling together helps to make a wolf pack stronger.*

Threatening growl

Wolves don't just howl—they bark and whimper, too. Wolves also growl, just like domestic dogs. They pull back their lips to bare their teeth and make a deep, rumbling growl. This is usually a warning sound. An alpha wolf uses a growl to threaten others.

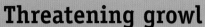 *A growling wolf bares its teeth as a warning to others to stay away. It growls to protect young, defend the pack territory, and keep scavengers away from a fresh kill.*

Barking for help

Wolves bark just like dogs. A nervous wolf may make a quiet bark, but usually a bark is used as a warning or an alarm to alert other pack members to possible danger. Sometimes, a wolf adds a bark to the end of a howl. Pups also do this to get their mother's attention when they are hungry. An older wolf does a bark-howl when it is scared or distressed.

FACT

The wolves that live in countries of the Middle East, such as Saudi Arabia and Iran, do not howl.

Life Cycle

Only the alpha female in a pack has pups. The rest of the pack help her feed and guard the young to make sure that as many as possible survive.

A safe den

The alpha female usually mates with the alpha male. If the alpha male is closely related, she mates with one of the beta wolves. In spring, she gives birth to as many as seven pups that are born in the safety of a den. The den is usually a large hole that has been dug out by the pack, but sometimes the female chooses a cave or a hole under a tree. The den is always found near the center of the territory, well away from other packs.

These gray wolf pups are greedily feeding on their mother's milk.

Deaf and blind

The pups are born deaf and blind, and huddle together for warmth. Their eyes open after about 12 days, and they start to move around. After about three weeks, their ears unfold. By the time they are a month old, the pups are ready to explore outside the den and meet the rest of the pack. During this time, the pack guards the den and brings food for the mother. The pups feed on the mother's milk for about two months and then start to eat meat.

These wolf cubs are blind and deaf. They are living in the safety of the den.

FACT

Life is tough for wolf cubs, and about half die during their first year. This may be because of a lack of food, disease, or injury. Some wolf cubs are killed by other predators or humans.

Play fighting

Young wolf pups are very curious and want to learn more about their surroundings. It is important for them to bond with the rest of the pack. Pretend fights with each other help them to do this. Play fighting helps the pups become stronger, teaches them how to defend themselves, and develops their hunting skills without getting hurt.

Wolf pups learn how to bite while they play. If they bite too hard, the other pup yelps!

Adult wolves play, too. They have mock fights in which they chase each other around and jump on top of each other.

FACT

Place in the pack

When a pup wants to play with another, it crouches down and wags it tail. Pups will chase and bite each other, and roll around together squealing and growling, but they don't hurt each other when they play. By the time they are five weeks old, the pups have already worked out their position in the litter.

These young wolves are eagerly following an adult on a hunt. They watch the kill but won't join in until they are older.

Leaving the pack

When the pups are three or four months old, they follow the pack and start to hunt, but they still need their mother to give them food. By the time they are nine months old, they will have made their first kill. Some of the youngsters, especially the males, leave the pack when they are one year old, while others will remain with the pack for life. Wolves are ready to breed when they are about two years old.

When pups are hungry, they lick the muzzle of adults returning from a hunt, hoping that the adult will regurgitate some food.

The Future of Wolves

Wolves are threatened around the world. Their numbers have fallen dramatically, and in some places, the wolf has disappeared completely.

Before the hunting of wolves was made illegal, wolf pelts or skins were openly sold in street markets. They were used to make coats and rugs.

Hunted

Wolves have been hunted for hundreds of years. Farmers have shot, poisoned, and trapped wolves to protect their herds from attack. In Central Asia, wolves are still shot for their fur. There has also been a loss of wolf habitat, especially in places such as Ethiopia where people are clearing more land for farming.

▶| *In Central Europe, trained dogs are used to protect flocks of sheep from wolf attacks.*

Disappeared

The gray wolf has virtually disappeared from Western Europe, much of the United States, Mexico, and China. Elsewhere, its numbers are low. By 1970, wolf numbers were so low that many countries decided to protect them, making it illegal to kill wolves. Their numbers have increased slowly since then.

Red wolf

The red wolf is on the edge of extinction. By 1980, it was extinct in the wild but bred in zoos. In 1987, some captive-bred red wolves were released into North Carolina, where they are thriving. There are about 100 red wolves now living in the wild, so there is hope that wild packs will continue to grow.

Save the wolf

Many conservation organizations are working around the world to protect wolves. In some places, wolves have been reintroduced to areas where they once roamed in large numbers. In Yellowstone National Park, elk (a type of large deer) increased in number so much that they were damaging forests and producing weak offspring. The elk population was controlled by reintroducing their natural predator, the wolf.

▼ *This red wolf is being released back into the wild in the state of North Carolina.*

Not popular

In Europe, there are plans to reintroduce the wolf to parts of Scotland. However, reintroductions are often unpopular and not everybody welcomes the return of wolves, especially farmers. They fear that if wolf numbers grow, their farm animals will be threatened once again.

Sixty-six wolves were released into Yellowstone National Park in 1995, and by 2005, there were about 900 wolves living there.

FACT

Wolf watching

Wolves are popular with tourists. Each year, about 100,000 people visit Yellowstone National Park just to see the wolves, while 10,000 people join in the wolf howl program in Algonquin Provincial Park, Canada. The red wolves in North Carolina are popular, too. Tourists are important because they bring money into an area and create jobs. This encourages local people to conserve the wolf.

These tourists are watching a pack of captive wolves in Denmark.

43

Facts and Records

🐾 The largest gray wolves are the Arctic wolves. The males are about 6 ft. 6 in. (2 m) long (from nose to tail), stand about 30 in. (76 cm) at the shoulder, and weigh up to 176 lbs. (80 kg). The females are about one-fifth smaller.

🐾 The red wolf is 4 ft. (1.2 m) long (from nose to tail) and weighs between 40 and 80 lbs. (18 and 36 kg). It stands about 26 in. (66 cm) at the shoulder.

🐾 Wolves are nearsighted and cannot see well beyond 75 ft. (23 m), so they rely more on their hearing and sense of smell.

🐾 Young wolves reach adult size by the time they are six months old.

🐾 Female wolves eat more slowly than the males.

🐾 The wolf has a narrow chest, which is useful in snowy conditions, when they can push through deep snow like a snow plow.

🐾 A wolf's howl lasts from a fraction of a second to 12 seconds. With the right weather conditions, howls can be heard from a distance of more than 9 mi. (15 km).

🐾 A wolf usually chases its prey for up to 220 yds. (200 m) and then gives up, but in one case a wolf was known to chase a moose for 20 mi. (32 km).

🐾 The gray wolf lives 8–10 years in the wild, and as much as 20 years in captivity. The red wolf has a slightly shorter life span of 6–8 years.

◀ *There are fewer than 500 Ethiopian wolves left in the wild.*

An average pack size of gray wolves is 5-7 members, not including pups.

🐾 The Ethiopian wolf has many other names including the Simian wolf, Abyssinian wolf, red jackal, Simian jackal, and Horse's jackal. The males weigh between 33 and 42 lbs. (15 and 19 kg) and they are larger than the females.

Wolves walk at about 4 mph (6.4 kph).

🐾 The maned wolf looks a bit like a wolf, but it is not a true wolf. It is a member of the dog family, like the fox and coyote.

🐾 In 1833, Charles Darwin visited the Falkland Islands and studied the Falkland Island wolves. Sadly, by 1883, the wolves became extinct.

🐾 A female gray wolf is pregnant for about two months, and she gives birth to up to 11 pups. The largest recorded litter contained 17 pups. A newborn pup weighs just 1 lb. (0.5 kg).

🐾 The coat of a gray wolf is made up of white, red, brown, and black colored hairs. Some gray wolves are completely black, while others are pure white. Black wolves are rarely seen outside of North America and Italy.

🐾 Wolves have scent glands between their toes, and they leave a smell on the ground that other wolves can follow.

Glossary

Aborigines The first people to live in Australia.

Alpha wolf The top wolf in a pack.

Beta wolf The second wolf in a pack.

Bone marrow The soft material in the middle of a large bone.

Camouflage Coloring that helps an animal to blend with its surroundings so it is hard to see.

Caribou A type of deer, called reindeer in Europe.

Carnivore A type of mammal, such as a cat or dog, that eats meat.

Conservation Saving, protecting, and managing habitats that are under threat.

Dominant Top; having a controlling role.

Extinct No longer in existence; a species that has died out.

Insulation A covering that keeps an animal warm, such as hair or fat.

Interact To act and communicate together.

Mammal A type of animal that feeds its young milk and is usually covered in hair.

Moose A type of large deer; the male has enormous flat antlers.

Northern hemisphere Part of the Earth to the north of the equator.

Offspring Young or pups.

Omega The last wolf in a pack.

Pad The cushion-like underside of a wolf's foot.

Predator An animal that hunts other animals for food.

Saliva Watery liquid produced in the mouth.

Scavenge To feed on dead matter, such as the remains of dead animals.

Submissive Meek; willing to follow the wishes of another.

Tundra Treeless plains in the Arctic where the ground is permanently frozen.

Urine Liquid waste produced by an animal.

Index